E

Epstein, Samuel

Mister Peale's
mammoth

# MISTER PEALE'S
# MAMMOTH

# MISTER PEALE'S
# MAMMOTH

by Sam and Beryl Epstein

illustrated by Martim Avillez

Coward, McCann & Geoghegan, Inc.   New York

For F. P.
with affection and thanks from us both

Library of Congress Cataloging in Publication Data
Epstein, Samuel, 1909–    Mister Peale's mammoth.
Bibliography: p.
SUMMARY: Enthralled by the new science of natural history, a famous American painter establishes a museum in his home and organizes a scientific expedition to find and dig up a complete mammoth skeleton.
1.  Peale, Charles Willson, 1741-1827—Juvenile fiction. [1. Peale, Charles Willson, 1741-1827—Fiction. 2. Mammoth —Fiction] I. Epstein, Beryl Williams, 1910-joint author.  II. Avillez, Martim. III. Title.
PZ7.E7252Mi  [Fic]  76-49644
ISBN 0-698-20402-6   ISBN 0-698-30647-3 lib. bdg.
Printed in the United States of America

# CONTENTS

# I

# The Big Bones

Mr. Peale did the family marketing early that summer morning in 1783, because he expected the bones to arrive that very day. His long legs carried him swiftly back from Philadelphia's busy Market Street to his brick house on the corner of Third and Lombard.

There, in his carpentry room, Charles Willson Peale repaired the hinge of his mother's set of false teeth. (He himself had carved them for her, out of ivory.)

Then, in his painting room, he put the finishing touches on his portrait of General Henry Knox. At last he was ready for the final chore he wanted done before the bones came. He went into his gallery to decide where General Knox should hang.

Mr. Peale was proud of the long high room, with its row of windows in the slanted roof to serve as a skylight. It was the first art gallery in America. Already there were more than thirty portraits on its walls. Mr. Peale had painted them so that Americans could become acquainted with George Washington, Lafayette, and the other heroes of their new land.

Now he looked around at the painted faces. He had fought beside many of these men and knew them all. If he moved Tom Paine a foot or so to the right, he thought, General Knox could be hung beside him.

At that moment his young son Rembrandt shouted from the gallery doorway. "Pa! The man is here with the big bones!"

"Then General Knox will just have to wait," Mr. Peale muttered to himself. To Rembrandt he said, "We'll put them in the painting room. Bring Raphaelle and Angelica there so that you can all watch me unpack them."

Mr. Peale took for granted that his children, each named after a famous painter, would be interested in everything that interested him.

He was rubbing his hands happily together as he strode off. He knew he was going to enjoy the work ahead of him because he had never made drawings of bones before. There was no greater pleasure, Mr. Peale always thought, than trying something new.

But there was another reason for his satisfaction this morning. His drawings were going to be paid for! And though with the long War for Independence just over, money was scarce for many people, it had always been scarce for Mr. Peale. Somehow, even now that he had become the best-known painter in America, he was still regularly out of blast, as he put it.

Five minutes later, in his painting room, he was carefully lifting the bones out of the baskets and casks they had been delivered in.

"This is a legbone," he told the children as he lowered one large object to the floor.

"But it's so big!" Raphaelle said. "It's almost as big as Rembrandt!"

All three of the children were staring at it.

"And this is part of an upper jawbone," Mr. Peale said next. "Those big lumps on it are molars—the kind of teeth you have in the back of your mouth, the ones you chew with."

Angelica touched one of her own teeth. It was no larger than the end of her finger. Then she stretched her hands toward one of the big molars. It was as large as both her fists together. She pulled her hands back quickly.

"Are these the bones of a giant, Pa?" she asked. She sounded a little scared.

Her father shook his head. "They're the bones of a big animal—an animal that died a long time ago."

"What kind of animal?" Raphaelle wanted to know.

"No one can answer that question," his father told him. "A good many bones like these have been found here and there in America. These and some broken pieces of tusks came from the bank of the Ohio River. An Indian trader picked them up there. But no one has ever found all the bones of a big skeleton lying together, so no one knows what sort of shape the animal had."

"If it had tusks, it must have been an elephant," nine-year-old Raphaelle said confidently. He liked to display his superior knowledge before his younger brother and sister.

"But scientists say no elephant could have lived in our American climate," his father said. "And they say these aren't elephant teeth," he added, pointing to the big molars. "They say these are like the teeth of a hippopotamus."

"But a hippopotamus doesn't have tusks!" Raphaelle said.

"That's so," Mr. Peale agreed. "And that is why no one knows what kind of animal these bones belonged to. Perhaps it is an animal no one has ever seen."

"Maybe," Rembrandt said, "a man will go exploring someday, and he will find an animal walking around in the woods, and that animal will have big bones like these. Then we'll know what it looks like."

His father nodded. "Many people hope that will happen," he said. "But most of the men who have studied bones like these don't think it will. They say that for some reason they can't explain, no animals with bones like these are alive today anywhere."

The men Mr. Peale meant were pioneers of a new science called natural history. They no longer believed what most people still believed—that God had created the earth and all its creatures in a single week, as the Bible said, and that nothing had changed since that time.

None of these scientists had yet figured out the theory of evolution, the idea that _living_ things can evolve, or change, and even die out. It would be seventy-five years before Charles Darwin announced that theory. But even in Mr. Peale's time the men who were studying nature very carefully were coming

close to discovering the idea of a constantly changing world.

Angelica was looking from one big bone to another. "Poor animal!" she said. "Doesn't it even have a name?"

"Some people are calling it the American Incognitum," her father said. "That means the American Unknown. But others are calling it the American mammoth, because they think it may have been like the Siberian mammoth.

"Mind you," he added, "no one has ever seen a live Siberian mammoth either. But the whole skeleton of a big animal, with tusks, was dug up in Siberia not long ago and given that name."

"Did the Siberian mammoth have bones as large as these?" Raphaelle asked.

"I don't know," Mr. Peale said.

He certainly hoped it didn't. He had been annoyed when a
French scientist, the Count Buffon, declared that all animals in
America were smaller than the animals of other continents. Mr.
Peale wished someone would prove Count Buffon wrong. Mr.
Peale was the kind of American who wanted his new country
to have the biggest and best of everything.

By now he had all the bones spread out on the floor. He
studied them for a moment and decided to draw the legbone
first.

"Bring me some sheets of drawing paper from the cup-
board," he told Raphaelle. Then, with Rembrandt and

14

Angelica in tow, Mr. Peale went to the kitchen to make a pot of paste.

Not long afterward they were all back in the painting room. Raphaelle helped his father lay several sheets of paper end to end on the floor, beside the big legbone, until they made a row as long as the bone.

Then Mr. Peale used the gooey paste he had made to stick the sheets together. Finally, on that long strip of paper, he started to draw a picture of the bone that would be the same size as the bone itself.

"Why are you making a picture of it, Pa?" Rembrandt asked.

"Because the man who owns these bones doesn't want to

send them to Europe," Mr. Peale said. "So my drawings of them will be sent instead. In Europe they will be studied by natural history scientists."

"Aren't there any of those scientists in America?" Raphaelle asked.

"America doesn't have large universities like those in Europe," Mr. Peale said, "and that is where the best scientific study goes on. But," he added quickly, "someday America will have many universities of its own. And I have no doubt they will be as large and fine as any in all the world."

In the weeks **that** followed, Mr. Peale made almost forty drawings of the big bones. He drew the legbone, for example, first from one side and then from the other. Then he made a drawing of each end. Anyone seeing those drawings would know exactly what that bone looked like.

One day he had a visit from his good friend and brother-in-law, Nathaniel Ramsey. When Mr. Ramsey saw the bones, he became very excited. He looked at them for a long time, shaking his head in amazement. Finally he said, "I would have gone twenty miles to see such a collection!"

Then, suddenly, Mr. Ramsey declared that he knew how Mr. Peale could make lots of money—the one thing Mr. Peale always seemed to need. Mr. Peale, he said, should have displays of old bones and other curiosities in his gallery and charge admission to see them. Then he'd be in blast sure enough!

Mr. Peale nodded thoughtfully. It was an interesting idea.

On the other hand, he reminded his brother-in-law, painting was his business. And even if he didn't sell as many pictures as he might wish, he had lately had several orders for copies of certain portraits in his gallery. John Hancock, for example, had ordered a copy of Mr. Peale's portrait of Washington. The French ambassador had ordered another and would present his copy to the king of France. Mr. Peale would thus be the first American painter to have his work hanging in the French royal palace.

So Mr. Peale thanked Mr. Ramsey for his well-meant suggestion, and that seemed to be the end of that. When Mr. Ramsey left, Mr. Peale pushed the whole idea to the back of his mind.

But there the idea grew. And grew.

And one day several years later he called his family together and announced, "We are going to have a museum in the gallery!"

He said it wouldn't be in the least like the few museums already existing in America. Those places held only a jumble, a hodgepodge of objects. In the Peale Museum, he said, everything would be arranged in order according to the plan set forth by the great Swedish scientist Linnaeus. Linnaeus, he said, had recently shown that there was order in all nature, that every plant and animal belonged to a family of similar plants and animals.

"So we shall show everything in its proper family group," Mr. Peale said. "People who visit our museum will be able to learn all about the wonders of the world and especially about the wonders of our own new land. Our museum will be a true School of Nature!"

# II
# Mr. Peale's Museum

On a July morning in 1786 Mr. Peale was busy painting a land-scape on his gallery wall. It was a marshy scene, with blue sky above it. When his brother James came in, from his own home a few doors along Lombard Street, he eyed it admiringly. James knew a good piece of work when he saw it. He too was a painter. Mr. Peale had taught him years before, just as he was now teaching Rembrandt and Raphaelle.

"This will be the background for a display of the ducks I shot in the marsh last month," Mr. Peale said, waving his brush at it. "They will be set among real clumps of grass, around the mirror that will represent a pond. In that way I can show what sort of place the ducks inhabit."

"Splendid!" James said. Only his brother, he felt, could even think of designing such a display. It would be a lesson in natural history and at the same time it would be as pretty as a picture. "Your announcement is splendid too, Charles," he added, and handed Mr. Peale that day's *Pennsylvania Packet*.

Mr. Peale was smiling as he put down his brush and adjusted

his spectacles. He did enjoy seeing his own words in print. His newspaper announcement began:

MR. PEALE, ever desirous to please and entertain the Public, will make a part of his House a Repository for Natural Curiosities. The Public he hopes will thereby be gratified in the sight of many of the Wonderful Works of Nature . . . .

"It was wise of you, Charles," James said when Mr. Peale put the paper down, "to say only that you wish to 'please and entertain' the public."

"I chose the words most carefully," Mr. Peale told him. "Had I said I wished to educate people, they might be frightened away."

"And no doubt you also chose carefully those words asking friends to assist you with the museum," James said, pointing to a phrase at the end of the newspaper announcement. "Do you believe people will really help you, Charles?"

James and Mr. Peale had already agreed to reduce the prices of their portraits in order to attract more customers and make as much money as possible. But they both knew they could never make enough to build a museum on their own.

"I do indeed count on help," Mr. Peale assured his brother. "I count especially on our friends in the American Philosophical Society."

Mr. Peale had just been invited to join the remarkable society he was talking about. Benjamin Franklin had started it. He had brought doctors, lawyers, farmers, merchants, artisans, and craftsmen together and urged them to learn from one another. Thus, he said, they would "improve the common stock of knowledge." And since the word "philosophy" was then generally used to cover the whole world of knowledge, Dr. Franklin had called it the American Philosophical Society.

Its members had already helped create the University of the State of Pennsylvania, the first university in America. Mr. Peale was sure they would help create his museum, too. In the meantime he was getting on with it as best he could himself.

Half an hour later James was at work at his slanted desk. Using a magnifying glass, he was painting on ivory a tiny portrait called a miniature. It had been ordered for a young lady who would wear it as a locket.

Mr. Peale, on his hands and knees, was studying the display he had just arranged.

The mirror, he thought, really shimmered like water in the sunshine flooding down on it from the skylight. The grass he had painted on the wall behind the mirror looked as real as the twelve clumps of real grass he had set around it. Among the grass clumps were the eight ducks he had finished mounting only the night before.

Carefully he fluffed up one duck's feathers. Then he moved another duck a bit closer to a clump of grass. Yes, that was better! Now the stuffed birds looked almost exactly like eight live ones resting on the grassy edge of a pond.

Mr. Peale hoped the birds would go on looking as good as they did at this moment. He couldn't be sure they would. He had removed their skins with the tools he had at hand. Before stuffing them he had soaked them in turpentine from his painting supplies. He had no idea whether that would preserve them or not, and he could ask no one for advice. There was not a single taxidermist among all of Philadelphia's thousands of craftsmen.

"Pa!" Raphaelle had burst into the gallery. "See what Dr. Franklin sent you! A dead cat! His Angora cat!"

Mr. Peale got quickly to his feet, brushing off the knees of his brown breeches. He looked happily down at the limp furry body in the basket Raphaelle held.

"Did you hear, James?" he asked. "Dr. Franklin himself has sent us a contribution! Now there can be no doubt at all that our museum will be a great success!"

As it turned out, Mr. Peale had to bury the corpse of Dr. Franklin's cat a week or so later. His attempt to preserve it had failed completely. And before the summer was over, he also had to destroy the ducks he had soaked in turpentine. Insects had chewed them up.

But Mr. Peale kept trying. Month after month he went on stubbornly experimenting until he became an expert taxidermist.

He learned to soak certain specimens in a big kettle of arsenic solution he brewed in his backyard. The poison left sores on his hands and made him sick. His wife, Rachel, begged him not

to touch it again. He couldn't listen to her. Arsenic, he said, was the best thing for preserving his birds and small animals.

For larger animals he used a solution of mercury, another dangerous poison. And to make those animals look as lifelike as possible, he first carved animal figures out of wood, with every muscle showing, and then fitted the skins tightly over them.

Slowly the museum was taking shape. Gifts for it arrived steadily. One was a pair of golden pheasants Lafayette had sent to General Washington. They had died soon after they arrived from France, and the general had given them to Mr. Peale.

Finally, in July, 1788, Mr. Peale put an announcement in the *Packet* to say his museum was officially open. Tickets of admission, the announcement said, would cost one shilling.

Life was busier for the whole Peale family after that. Someone always had to be at the door to sell tickets and to warn visitors not to touch the stuffed birds that had been treated with arsenic. Someone else had to be on hand to answer questions. Mr. Peale liked to do that job himself if he had the time.

He always wanted to make sure that visitors saw the grotto he had made out of imitation rock, where he displayed some of his stuffed snakes. He had set up a magnifying glass in front of one of the rattlesnakes, so that people could clearly see its fangs and its poison ducts.

His portraits of Revolutionary heroes were part of the museum too. They still helped Americans understand what kind of men those heroes were. But now, Mr. Peale said, the portraits also represented *Genus homo,* or man. And he liked to tell people what Linnaeus had said: that human beings belonged to a family of animals called primates—along with monkeys, chimpanzees, and gorillas. Some visitors were so shocked to hear him call man an animal that they walked out and never came back.

People who came to the museum especially enjoyed seeing

Mr. Peale's backyard. There he kept the young birds and animals he didn't want to kill and mount until they were fully grown. There he also kept the "freaks of nature" he was

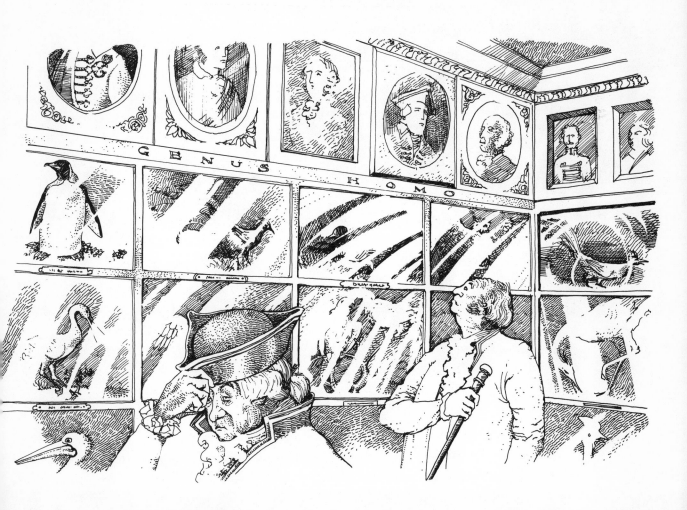

sometimes given. Among them was a cow with two tails, five legs, and six feet.

Mr. Peale didn't really want to have those freaks in his

museum. He wanted to teach people about the normal world of nature, not amaze them with nature's accidents. But the freaks did attract crowds, and now every visitor meant one more shilling in his pocket. And Mr. Peale was still out of blast. The shillings coming in were never enough to support his family and pay for all the things he wanted for new displays.

His brother-in-law, Mr. Ramsey, tried to be helpful. The museum would attract more paying customers, he declared, if it showed some big bones like the ones he'd seen years before in Mr. Peale's own house.

Mr. Peale said he was sure Mr. Ramsey was right, but such curiosities weren't easy to come by. Mr. Peale didn't even mention his own hope that he might someday be able to display an entire skeleton of an American Incognitum. He wasn't the most practical man in the world, but he did know that was more a dream than a possibility.

He had been using a good deal of energy lately, trying to get support for his museum from the new United States government. So far he had had no success. And even Thomas Jefferson, fellow member of the Philosophical Society and a good friend of the museum, said he was unlikely ever to succeed.

Then help of an unexpected kind suddenly came to Mr. Peale.

The society had just built a handsome brick and marble building in State House Square, now called Independence Square, in the heart of Philadelphia. And since the society would need only two rooms for its own use, it rented the rest, and the grounds around the building, to Mr. Peale. The society also asked him to take charge of its own collection of scientific curiosities and display it in his museum.

At one stroke the museum was receiving new exhibits and better and bigger space for displays. And the Peale family would have bigger and better living quarters in the same building. The society even put a kitchen in the cellar for the family's use.

The Peales moved into the American Philosophical Society Hall one summer day in 1794, before the museum itself was moved. They had been through some sad times during recent years. Mr. Peale's mother had died. So had his dear wife, Rachel.

But things had taken a more cheerful turn even before the Peales settled in their strange new home. Angelica was marrying a handsome English-born gentleman. The rest of Rachel's children loved their new young stepmother, Betsy. And everyone loved Betsy's new baby.

To the surprise of Mr. Peale's friends, he hadn't named the baby after a famous artist. Instead the child was named Charles, after himself, perhaps because Betsy insisted, and Linnaeus for the Swedish scientist Mr. Peale so much admired. Young Charles Linnaeus proved to the world that Mr. Peale's enthusiasm for painting had been swallowed up by his newer enthusiasm for the science of natural history.

Finally came moving day for the museum. Mr. Peale hired men with hand barrows to carry glass exhibit cases and other breakable things. But he invited his friends and all the boys in the neighborhood to help move the rest. They formed a great parade such as Philadelphia had never seen before.

The procession started with the museum's American buffalo, so big that several men had to carry it on their shoulders. Behind it came boys with the smaller creatures.

There was a bear, a leopard, and a tiger.

There was an anteater.

There were deer, wildcats, foxes, raccoons, and opossums. There were rabbits and squirrels.

There were turtles, frogs, lizards, and toads.

There were ducks, geese, cranes, herons, and other water birds.

There were rattlesnakes, black snakes, glass snakes, and striped snakes.

There were the wax figures Mr. Peale had made so that he could display the Indian and Tahitian costumes he had been given. There were shields and bows and arrows.

And last there were all the live creatures of the backyard menagerie—eagles, owls, baboons, monkeys, one bear, and the cow with two heads, five legs, and six feet.

The museum's displays looked fine in their new home. The creatures of the menagerie roamed happily in a fenced-off portion of the grounds.

One visitor said, "I have seen the two greatest museums in Europe, Mr. Peale—the one in London and the one in Paris. And I can assure you that your museum compares favorably with them both."

"Thank you, sir," Mr. Peale said, but he couldn't keep the testiness out of his voice.

"Compares favorably!" That wasn't good enough for him, and it wasn't good enough for his country. He wanted America's first and only real museum of natural history to be the best museum of all.

Sometimes he still thought wistfully of the one exhibit that would make it world-famous overnight—if only he could obtain it: the skeleton of an American Incognitum or American mammoth. How glorious it would be to display such a thing! he thought. How many thousands of people would flock to see it! And how sad it was that such a skeleton had never yet been found.

More huge bones and teeth and pieces of tusks had been turning up lately, usually in Ohio or New York. More and more commonly they were being called mammoth bones. Thanks to the Philosophical Society, Mr. Peale even had a few

mammoth teeth on display, and everyone who came to the museum gazed at them with awe.

But a few teeth were a far cry from a whole skeleton—a mighty far cry indeed.

Early in 1801 Thomas Jefferson, then president of the Philosophical Society, became President of the United States. He would live in the capital, which had already been moved from Philadelphia to the new city of Washington. But Mr. Jefferson's heart was still with the society and what it believed in and supported. And to Mr. Peale the election of his friend Jefferson to the highest office in the land seemed a good omen for the museum.

In June of that same year Mr. Peale read a newspaper account that brought him up out of his chair. It said that dozens and dozens of mammoth bones had been found on a farm in New York State. For all Mr. Peale knew, they might even be all the bones of a complete skeleton!

"I must go there!" he said. "At once!"

And at once he set out. After a two-day stagecoach journey to New York City and a seventy-mile sail by sloop up the Hudson River, he rode a wagon to the home of a Dr. George Graham. Dr. Graham lived near the farm of John Masten, where the bones had been found. He welcomed Mr. Peale warmly and had a great deal to tell him on their first evening together. Not all of it was good news.

# III
# More Big Bones

The mammoth bones, Dr. Graham said, had been discovered in a swampy patch of marl on the Masten farm. Mr. Peale knew marl was a sort of clay farmers used to enrich their fields.

"Masten was digging up marl when he found them," Dr. Graham explained. "He told his neighbors about the bones. And the first thing you know, the neighbors were looking for more bones in Masten's marl. They brought plenty of grog along and made a sport of their digging. They took no care to keep the bones whole or to see how they lay."

"But someone should have sketched the bones before they were moved!" Mr. Peale said.

"Aye," Dr. Graham agreed. "But no one thought of that. And when the pit they dug began to fill with water, they grew tired of the sport and gave it up. Now the bones lie helter-skelter in Masten's barn, and his only wish is to make as much money from them as possible."

The next morning Dr. Graham drove Mr. Peale to the Masten farm, and Mr. Peale had his first sight of the bones. If they were properly arranged, he thought they might indeed form a complete skeleton!

He was tempted to make an offer for them right on the spot. He had brought $300 with him, a sum larger than many workmen earned in a year. He was willing to spend all of it in the hope of obtaining a mammoth skeleton for the museum. But he knew it was wise not to seem too eager. If Masten were willing to sell, he thought, the man would certainly let him know.

"Would you object if I made drawings of the bones?" Mr. Peale asked.

Masten seemed to have little interest in what his visitor wanted to do. Mr. Peale fetched his drawing kit and set to work.

He didn't have to stop to figure out how to do this job. Just as he had done eighteen years before, he first pasted sheets of paper together to make strips and squares as large as he needed. Then, with the greatest possible care, he started to draw the exact images of the bones and pieces of bone that lay scattered around him.

As he worked, he realized that a complete skeleton could never be put together out of the bones in the barn. There was no lower jawbone, for example, and not enough broken pieces to form a complete skull. Therefore, it would be impossible even to guess at the shape of the mammoth's head.

Mr. Peale wondered if the missing pieces still lay buried in the flooded marl pit. He wanted very much to dig in that pit himself.

Masten came into the barn from time to time, but he didn't say a word about selling the bones. And Mr. Peale had resolved not to speak first.

Then, on the day the drawings were nearly finished, Masten said, "Would you be interested in buying these bones, Mr. Peale?"

Mr. Peale took a deep breath. "Yes," he said. "I think I would."

"How much do you figure to pay for them?" Masten asked.

Mr. Peale hesitated. He could no longer afford to spend all his money for the bones in the barn. Now he wanted something else besides.

"I will give you two hundred dollars for the bones," he said. "And one hundred dollars more for permission to dig in your marl pit."

Masten shook his head. "I could make more than that by taking the bones from town to town and showing them off in taverns."

Mr. Peale said he thought exhibits in taverns might not prove that profitable. Masten didn't reply. He simply walked away.

The next day Mr. Peale came sadly back to the barn to pick up his drawings and his drawing kit. Suddenly the farmer was beside him.

"I've been thinking about your offer, Mr. Peale," he said. "I'll take it."

Mr. Peale's heart "jumped for joy," as he wrote his wife that night.

Masten could see how pleased Mr. Peale was. "But I would like a bit extra—something to boot," he added quickly. "I'd like a bird gun like the one you have and some gowns for my daughters."

Mr. Peale agreed. The men shook hands on the deal.

With great care Mr. Peale packed the bones in two large casks and two barrels. Only the thighbone, too big to fit into even the largest cask, had to be left behind temporarily. In hired wagons he carted all the others to the river and started them on their slow trip by water to Philadelphia and the museum.

Then he left for home himself, taking a stagecoach for a faster journey.

By the time he reached Philadelphia Mr. Peale had decided that he wanted to organize an expedition to search for a complete skeleton of a mammoth. If the expedition were successful, every natural history scientist in the world would be grateful to him.

But Mr. Peale was an honest man. He admitted to himself that his chief purpose was to find a complete skeleton to exhibit in his museum. It would not only make the museum famous, but would also put him in blast for the rest of his life.

At the moment, having spent those $300, he was decidedly out of blast. He would have to borrow the money he needed. He made a formal request to the Philosophical Society for help.

The members studied the drawings he had made. They immediately voted to lend him $500.

Mr. Peale was ready to plan the first scientific expedition ever made in America.

# IV
# Hunting the Mammoth

In the first letter Mr. Peale wrote to President Jefferson after his return home, he asked to borrow a ship's pump and some military tents to use on his expedition. While he waited for an answer, the bones from Masten's farm arrived at the Philadelphia waterfront.

Mr. Peale hurried to the harbor. Others had heard the news and followed. Philadelphians knew that Mr. Peale had bought some bones of the great mammoth. Everyone was eager to see them.

The barrels and casks were loaded onto handcarts. Mr. Peale and his sons trundled them to the Philosophical Society Hall. There the bones were arranged on the museum floor.

"You can see that certain important parts are missing," Mr. Peale pointed out to his sons and to Mr. Fenton, who had recently been assisting him in the museum. All agreed about the importance of the missing lower jaw.

"Do you think it might yet be found in the pit?" Rembrandt asked.

"I think we must waste no time in starting a search for it," Mr. Peale said.

He was so eager to return to the Masten farm that he decided to leave even though he had not yet heard from President Jefferson. He borrowed a tent from the War Department. He knew he could buy other needed supplies on his way through New York City.

By the time the President's offer of help reached Philadelphia Mr. Peale was already setting up a camp beside the Masten marl pit. Rembrandt and Mr. Fenton were with him. So was a friend who was a chemistry professor. Mr. Peale's tent headquarters was large enough to hold all four men.

The first task of the expedition was to pump out the water that now filled the pit. The hand-operated pump Mr. Peale had brought from New York worked too slowly to suit him.

"We could empty the pit much faster if we used buckets fastened to a loop of rope," he said. "A turning wheel could keep the rope loop moving, sending the empty buckets down into the pit and bringing them up full of water. I've read that the Chinese use a wheel in that way to raise water from streams and canals for their fields."

Mr. Peale took a piece of paper and a pencil and began to sketch his idea. "We could build it like this," he said.

Soon he was setting a local carpenter and his crew to work. The men cut trees for lumber and then began to carry out Mr. Peale's plan. All day for several days the rasping of saws and the pounding of hammers and axes could be heard. People came from miles around to watch the queer goings-on at the Masten farm.

The wheel Mr. Peale and his carpenter's crew were building—they called it his Chinese wheel—stood twenty feet high. Several men could stand inside it on its four-foot-wide rim. Mr. Peale was always delighted to explain to curious onlookers how it would work.

If men standing inside the wheel "walked" steadily, he said, the wheel would keep turning on its huge log axle. And the turning wheel would turn the roller over which the big loop of rope would be hung. In this way the buckets fastened to the rope would be lowered into the pit and brought up filled with water. At the top of the loop, as the buckets passed over the roller, they would tip over, empty into a trough, and move down again.

By the time the strange contraption was finished dozens of onlookers wanted to help by "walking" the wheel. Several men at a time stood inside it, treading the rim so that the wheel turned. Down went the buckets. Up they came, to empty out and be sent down again. With other men working the hand pump at the same time, the water level in the pit fell rapidly. Soon there was only a shallow pool left.

Mr. Peale was looking happily down at that shallow pool when he saw that it was already growing deeper. This meant, he knew, that water was still seeping into the pit.

"We can begin our digging," he told Rembrandt and the others, "but we shall have to keep the pump going."

Now there were no longer volunteers eager to help. Keeping the hand pump going was hard work. Digging in the mud at the foot of the pit was even harder. Mr. Peale sent out word that he would hire twenty-five laborers.

"The pay will be nine shillings a day, New York money," he said.

That sum, worth $1.12, was a high daily wage for the time. A number of men appeared, more than willing to work for it. But after seeing that watery pit bottom, many of them turned away.

"Working down there would give a man a chill," one said.

"There will be daily rations of grog to warm you," Mr. Peale promised them. He didn't drink any alcohol himself, but he knew many people believed that the whiskey-and-water mixture called grog helped fight off chills. "And you will be paid at the end of each day's work," he added.

Twenty-five of the men agreed to work for him.

"Do not move any bones until I have seen them," Mr. Peale told his crew.

When he saw that the pit was so deep that the men couldn't heave the heavy marl over the rim, he had a platform built halfway up the pit wall. Then he divided his workers into two groups. One group threw the marl from the pit bottom to the platform. The other threw it from the platform up and over the rim.

Slowly the piles of marl around the edge of the pit grew taller. But no bones were found.

At last a cry rang out from the bottom of the pit. "Bones!"

Mr. Peale hurried down the ladder propped against the pit wall.

There, in the claylike mud, lay the bones of a complete foot, each in its proper place. Now, for the first time, Mr. Peale could see exactly how the animal's foot had been constructed. He opened his sketchbook and took out his pencil.

A warning shout halted his hand. The wall of the pit was slowly caving in under the great weight of the piles of marl on top. A mass of mud was creeping toward the bones.

Mr. Peale barely managed to snatch the larger bones out of the way before the rest were buried. His chance to sketch the shape of the foot had been lost.

The mud slide also meant that the digging had to be halted. All hands helped shift the piles of marl farther from the pit's edge. Then, as soon as the men returned to their digging, the pit wall began to collapse again.

And it went on collapsing, first at one point and then at another.

Mr. Peale had dozens of long poles driven into the bottom of the pit to form a wall against the moving mud. Once more the digging could go on.

From sunup to sundown, day after day, the work continued. Part of a tusk and a number of teeth were found. Parts of a skull were discovered, too, including parts of a lower jaw. But the bits of the jaw were not enough to show what its shape had been.

Each day Mr. Peale had to halt the digging so that the men could brace up the pit wall.

The soft ground caused other troubles, too. Suddenly the tall wooden framework that supported the Chinese wheel and its loop of buckets began to tilt over. Its log legs were sinking into the mud. The workmen scrambled out of the pit in fear for their lives.

Mr. Peale knew instantly how the framework could be saved. "Climb to the top and fasten a rope to it!" he ordered one of the men. "We'll brace it to that tree!"

The man looked at the shifting timbers and shook his head. "It will be down before I reach the top," he said.

Mr. Peale didn't waste time arguing. He snatched at the rope and scampered up the timber framework with the speed of a man half his sixty-year age. In seconds he had the rope tied to the timbers and was back on the ground again.

"Now take hold of the rope and pull!" he cried.

The men grabbed the rope and dug their heels into the ground. In a moment the tilting stopped. For another moment the framework hung motionless. Then slowly, under the pull of the rope, it began to straighten.

"Now!" Mr. Peale ordered, when it was upright again. "Make the rope fast to that tree!"

The framework was saved. Work could go on again.

But the work didn't turn up any more bones. Not that day and not the next day either.

Mr. Peale was discouraged. He felt he was wasting his bor-rowed money at the Masten farm. But he wasn't ready to re-

turn to Philadelphia. Dr. Graham had told him that some bones had been found in a swamp several miles away. The swamp's owner was willing for the expedition to try its luck on his property. Mr. Peale decided to keep only his best workmen and move his camp there.

The big Chinese wheel was taken apart. The bones were packed. The tent was pulled down. When everything was stowed in a big farm wagon, there was no room left for passengers. Mr. Peale and the others walked beside the wagon for its whole journey.

The new swampy area had to be drained before anything else could be done. Ditches were dug, and the hand pump was put to work.

While that labor was going on Mr. Peale developed a new tool—a long iron rod that could easily be pushed into the soft earth. He had several of them made, and he and the others practiced until they knew how a rod "felt" when it struck stone, wood, or bone.

The first several days' work with the rods turned up toebones, a backbone, two broken tusks, and many ribs. Then nothing more was found.

The owner of the swamp suggested another swampy place that might be worth trying. The expedition moved again.

Again the ditching and draining started. Three days of probing and digging produced only one small piece of backbone.

More than a month had now passed since Mr. Peale had left home. He had already spent far more than the sum the Philosophical Society had lent him.

"Shall we give up?" he asked Rembrandt and the others.

They talked it over. No one really wanted to return home with so little to show for their efforts. They especially hated the thought of leaving without a lower jawbone. And, of course, to leave now would mean Mr. Peale was giving up his dream of exhibiting a full mammoth skeleton in his museum. They agreed to try a little longer.

On September 7, after starting a new pit, they found a few scattered ribs.

For the next three days they moved slowly over the soggy ground, pushing the iron rods deep into it. They found nothing. But the wages of the workmen, who had no digging to do, still had to be paid.

As the morning of September 11 crept by, Mr. Peale and the others were once more stubbornly wielding their rods with no results. Mr. Peale was trying to accept the fact that the expedition was a costly failure. He knew he must bring it to an end before he went deeper into debt.

And then Mr. Fenton called out in a voice hoarse with excitement, "I feel bone!"

Rembrandt quickly joined him. Almost immediately he was shouting, "Yes! There is bone here!"

Mr. Peale hurried to the spot. He had scarcely pushed his rod into the ground when he was calling to the workmen, "Here! Dig here!"

Soon the shovels were scraping on something hard.

"Work slowly!" Mr. Peale said. "Take care!"

Part of a bone came into view. Mr. Peale bent over it and scraped the earth away with his hand. Moments later he and his men were lifting a huge shoulderbone out of the ground.

Legbones appeared next. Then, at long last, Mr. Peale was staring at the object he most wanted to see—a complete and unbroken lower jawbone!

The crew broke into cheers.

And then everybody went back to work again.

The bones they were now finding were often broken, but they did lie close together. Legbones were near footbones. One rib after another appeared.

By late afternoon of the next day, at the end of a row of neckbones, they discovered the spot where a skull had lain. It had crumbled away, leaving only a few scattered teeth. But, except for that missing skull, almost all the bones of a complete skeleton were now spread out beside their tent.

"We have accomplished even more than I had hoped," Mr. Peale said.

He still did not possess the top of a skull. But now he had at least one example, and in most cases two, of every other bone he had been seeking. And so, by carving copies of certain bones and contriving in some way or other a pair of skull tops, he would be able to put together not just one mammoth skeleton, but two!

One of them, he decided almost instantly, would be taken to Europe by Rembrandt and his young brother Rubens. There it could be seen by people who might have believed Count Buffon, and it would prove that Count Buffon had been wrong. No one could ever say again that the animals of America were smaller than those of other continents.

But the first skeleton that could be put together would be placed, of course, where Mr. Peale had so often dreamed it might stand—in Mr. Peale's Museum in the city of Philadelphia.

# V

# The Enormous Quadruped

Mr. Peale's Museum had never before been so full of excitement. The big bones were spread out on the floor in two groups, one for each of the skeletons that were to be put together. Mr. Peale and his crew went to work on one of them right away. They felt as if they were doing a giant jigsaw puzzle.

First the pieces of each broken bone had to be fitted together. It was slow work. Mr. Peale, Rembrandt, and Mr. Fenton were often discouraged. Sometimes it seemed they had tried every possible combination for joining a group of fragments.

Usually the bone fitters had an audience of onlookers eager to offer advice. Everyone in Philadelphia seemed to want to take part in creating the first American mammoth skeleton.

A lawyer, looking over Rembrandt's shoulder, might say, "That piece in your hand would fit there, below the joint."

"No, no!" a baker might argue. "Surely it belongs at the other end."

Then Moses Williams, a young slave in the Peale household, became interested. Moses—whom Mr. Peale planned to set free as soon as he could earn a living—proved to have remarkably skillful hands. He had sharp eyes, too. He saw ways of fitting broken bones together that no one else had thought of.

Finally, all the pieces of a skull had been put together except for the missing top. No one knew what the shape of that top should be.

"But we are sure the mammoth was like an elephant in many ways," Mr. Peale said. "Perhaps the top of his head was like that of an elephant."

So he studied the picture of an elephant in one of his books. Then he mixed a pot of paste and added many small pieces of paper to it. After stirring the mixture thoroughly, he let it rest for a time. When the paper was soft and soggy, the mixture had become the sticky substance the French call *papier-mâché*, or "chewed paper."

Then Mr. Peale shaped the *papier-mâché* into an imitation of the top of an elephant's skull. When it had dried and hardened, he set it in place in the hollow of the mammoth skull. It fitted perfectly. Finally he smoothed the *papier-mâché* and painted it the color of the mammoth bones. He was sure that anyone looking at it would be fooled into thinking he was seeing the whole real skull of a mammoth.

But Mr. Peale didn't want to fool people. So he drew a red line around the new top. The line would show, he said, that the part of the skull above it was "artificial." And he planned to put up a sign that would say just that.

54

Sometimes Mr. Peale sought help from Benjamin Rush, Philadelphia's famous sculptor. He showed Rush the two mammoth tusks that had been fitted together, each from several pieces. They were eleven feet long and strangely curved.

"We believe we have found the right shape for them," Mr. Peale said. "But they are too fragile to use. I would like to exhibit them in a glass case, where they would be safe from harm. Could you carve two wooden tusks to replace them on our skeleton?"

Rush carved the tusks and carved some small missing bones, too.

Finally, the time came to put the bones of the skeleton together.

Mr. Peale held the large legbones in place with iron hinges. He used iron rods to support the head, neckbones, backbone, ribs, and tailbones. He used thinner rods to hold the bones of the feet in place.

Slowly the great skeleton took shape. When it was finished, the space between its ribs measured six feet. It stood eleven feet high. And—not even counting those eleven-foot tusks—it was fifteen feet long.

For three months, ever since Mr. Peale's expedition had returned to the city, a sort of mammoth fever had been spreading in Philadelphia. It spread far outside the city, too. Mr. Peale had not discouraged it. In fact he had made sure that the *Packet* printed the reports he wrote about his mammoth. And he and his friends sent those reports to other newspapers all over the United States.

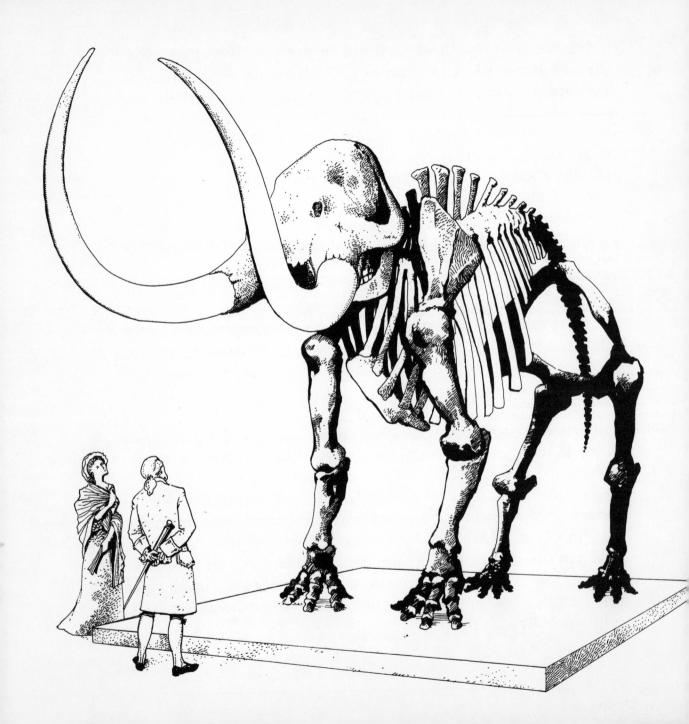

The word "mammoth" was becoming part of the language. One Philadelphia baker advertised his new large loaves as Mammoth Bread. A man in Washington ate forty-two eggs in ten minutes and claimed the title of Mammoth Eater. The town of Cheshire, in Massachusetts, sent a Mammoth Cheese to President Jefferson.

Philadelphians waited eagerly for their first view of the completed skeleton. Almost everyone agreed it would be worth the large price of fifty cents to see it. That was the fee Mr. Peale had decided to charge for admission to the special big room where the skeleton was set up.

More than six months had gone by since Mr. Peale had read that newspaper account of the bones found at the Masten farm. The year 1801 was almost over, but it was ending with a burst of glory for Mr. Peale. At Christmastime the Mammoth Room was finally ready to be opened to the public. The event had been announced in the newspapers. Boys had passed out hand-bills about it on the streets.

Moses Williams had the honor of conducting Philadelphians to their first view of the Great American Natural Wonder. He put on a tall Indian feather headdress and mounted a white horse. With a trumpeter blasting loudly ahead of him, he rode around Independence Square and up and down the city's cobbled streets. Children and grown-ups swarmed after him.

When the procession behind him was long enough, Moses led it to the museum. The doors swung open. Coins and paper money piled up on the admission table as men, women and children poured into the Mammoth Room.

There stood the skeleton of what Mr. Peale had called, in one of his newspaper accounts, "this ENORMOUS QUAD-RUPED . . . the LARGEST of Terrestrial Beings!"

No one who saw it that day, and none of the thousands of people who saw it in the years that followed, could ever forget the sight.

Mr. Peale's Mammoth, as people often called it, put him and his family happily in blast for the first time in their lives. And it did, indeed, as Mr. Peale had once dreamed, make his museum famous throughout the world.

# VI
# Afterward

And what happened afterward?

Well, Mr. Peale always had thought that trying something new was more interesting than doing the same thing over and over. As a young man he'd been a saddlemaker. At his first sight of a painting he'd known immediately that he must learn how to paint. Then he'd thrown himself into the great task of creating a natural history museum. Then he had organized a scientific mammoth-hunting expedition.

"I have misspent much of my time," he once wrote to his friend Thomas Jefferson. "A steady habit to any one object perhaps would have been more advantageous."

And indeed he didn't make "a steady habit" of seeking mammoth skeletons and learning all he could about them. It was a French scientist, Georges Cuvier, who carefully studied all the big bones he could manage to see and those drawings Mr. Peale had made so many years before. Cuvier learned that the great American animal and the great Siberian mammoth were not exactly alike. So it is Cuvier who is known today for

59

giving Mr. Peale's "mammoth" the name it now bears—the name "mastodon."

In the meantime Mr. Peale had left his son Rubens in charge of the museum and had "retired" to a farm he bought near Philadelphia.

There he invented a new kind of windmill and a cart that could carry milk, even over the bumpiest farm lane, without spilling it. He built a machine for planting corn and another for paring apples. He set up a greenhouse at the mouth of a cave, so that the warm air from the cavern could keep plants growing all winter.

In his seventies he was riding around his farm on a two-wheeled velocipede he had built. He had to walk it uphill and even on level ground. But downhill he could ride it, feet in the air, at flying speed.

Then suddenly, having picked up some of the new painting tricks Rembrandt had learned while he was showing the second "mammoth" skeleton in London, Mr. Peale took up his brushes again. The paintings he began to turn out were the best he had ever done. One was a large canvas he called "Exhuming the Mastodon." It shows for everyone to see, to this very day, all the excitement of that great search at the Masten marl pit.

There is the big Chinese wheel with its loop of buckets. There is the tall wooden supporting frame that Mr. Peale had saved from toppling over.

There are the laborers, digging in the deep pit. Around the pit's edge stand the curious onlookers from nearby farms, along with several of Mr. Peale's friends and many members of his family. Rembrandt was the only member of the family who had really been there, of course, but Mr. Peale enjoyed painting the others into the scene anyway.

And there is the tall erect figure of Mr. Peale himself. His right hand points down into the pit. His left hand holds up one end of a long strip of paper. There is a drawing on the paper that looks just like the one he started on that summer day in 1783 when it all began. It is the drawing of a very large, a really mammoth legbone.

# SELECTED BIBLIOGRAPHY

Bridenbaugh, Carl, *The Colonial Craftsman* (Chicago, University of Chicago Press, 1950) gives a clear picture of Philadelphia's craftsmen and artisans (Peale considered himself an artisan) during Peale's lifetime.

McLanathan, Richard, *The American Tradition in the Arts* (New York, Harcourt, Brace & World, 1968), another handsomely illustrated book, places Peale in his time—among the painters, sculptors, and architects of his day.

Sellers, Charles Coleman, *Charles Willson Peale* (New York, Charles Scribner's Sons, 1969). A large, handsomely illustrated book which tells the full story of Peale's life, his work, and the times. The author is a direct descendent of Peale's.

———, *Charles Willson Peale* (2 vols.) (Philadelphia, American Philosophical Society, 1947) is the basic source material for Sellers's later one-volume biography.

———, *Portraits and Miniatures by Charles Willson Peale* (Philadelphia, American Philosophical Society, 1952) reproduces in black and white illustrations hundreds of Peale's portraits and miniatures. Notes on the individual portraits give fascinating bits of information about the subject and in many cases his or her relationship with the artist. The notes about Peale's first portrait of George Washington, painted in 1772, include, for example, excerpts from Washington's diary during the days Peale spent at Mount Vernon: "May 20 . . . I sat to have my Picture drawn. May 21 . . . I sat again to take the Drapery. May 22. Sat for Mr. Peale to finish my face. In the afternoon Rid with him to my Mill."

————, *Charles Willson Peale with Patron and Populace* (Philadelphia, American Philosophical Society, 1969), a supplement to the above book, contains reproductions, in black and white, of Peale's landscapes, still lifes, sketches for inventions, and other drawings, along with more portraits and miniatures. In the notes for a set of drawings Peale made of the Hudson River during his first journey by sloop up that river is a paragraph from a letter he wrote at the time; he had been so "enraptured" by the "grand scene," he reported, that "I would, if I could, have made drawings with both hands at the same Instant."

The Charles Willson Peale collection in the Library of the American Philosophical Society, in Philadelphia, includes diaries, notes, and hundreds of letters in Peale's own hand.

# THE AUTHORS

From the moment Sam and Beryl Epstein learned about Charles Willson Peale, they found themselves enchanted by "this lively, ever-curious man, always so eager to explore the unknown, to try his hand at some new skill, and then to share his new knowledge with others."

Sam and Beryl Epstein have written books for both adult and young readers. The titles range over a wide variety of subjects that often required extensive research. Writing MISTER PEALE'S MAMMOTH included doing research at the beautiful library of the American Philosophical Society, the institution that helped Peale realize his dream of finding a complete mammoth skeleton.

Sam and Beryl live in Southold, New York.

# THE ARTIST

Martim Avillez is from Lisbon, Portugal, where he studied at the school of fine arts. He came to the United States in 1969, and was graduated from Cooper Union in New York City.

His illustrations have appeared in the New York *Times,* as well as in such periodicals as *Harper's Magazine* and *New York Magazine.*

Martim lives in New York City.